D0426654

Voices From The Past

VIETNAM WAR

KATHLYN GAY   MARTIN GAY

Twenty-First Century Books
Brookfield, Connecticut

Twenty-First Century Books
A Division of The Millbrook Press
2 Old New Milford Road
Brookfield, CT 06804

Text copyright © 1996 by Kathlyn Gay
All rights reserved.

Library of Congress Cataloging-in-Publication Data
Gay, Kathlyn.
Vietnam war / Kathly Gay and Martin Gay.—1st ed.
p. cm. — (Voices from the past)
Includes bibliographical references and index.
Summary: Provides an overview of the history of the
Vietnam War and U.S. involvement.
1. Vietnamese Conflict, 1961–1975—Juvenile literature.
[1. Vietnamese Conflict, 1961–1975.] I. Gay, Martin, 1950–   . II. Title.
III. Series: Gay, Kathlyn. Voices from the past.
DS557.7.G39   1996
959.704'3-dc20   96-15578
                                                            CIP
                                                            AC

ISBN 0-8050-4101-X

Printed in the United States of America

5 7 9 10 8 6

Cover design by Karen Quigley
Interior design by Kelly Soong

Cover: *Indiana Rangers: The Army Guard in Vietnam* by Mort Künstler
Courtesy of National Guard Heritage Series,
Dept. of the Army, National Guard Bureau, Washington, D.C.

Photo credits
pp. 7, 55: UPI/Corbis-Bettmann; pp. 9, 50,: Archive Photos; pp. 13, 21, 43: AP/
Wide World Photos; pp. 18, 33: Photri, Inc.; pp. 23, 46: James Pickerell/Black Star;
p. 27: Robert Ellison/Black Star; p. 36: Dick Swanson/Black Star; p. 39: Don
McCullin/Magnum Photos; p. 56: David Hume Kennerly/Black Star.

Contents

Bond #/World #llaWar

Property of Dexter
Middle School Library

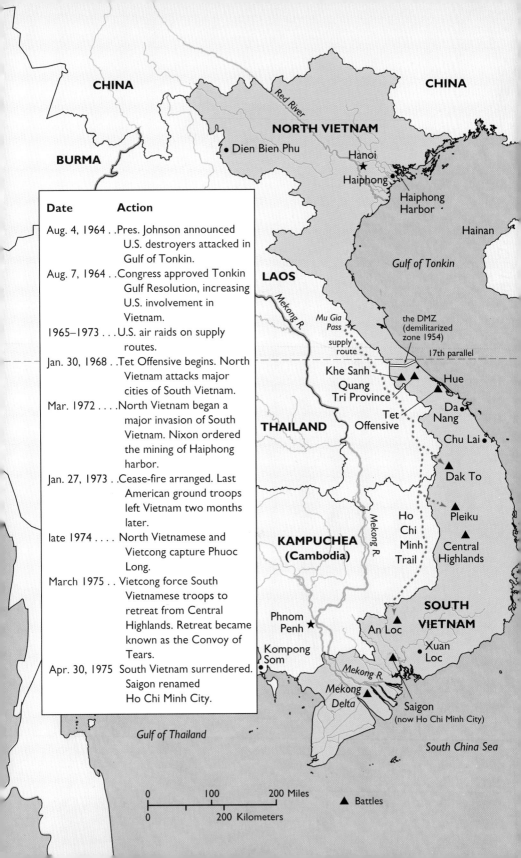

CHINA

CHINA

NORTH VIETNAM

Red River

• Dien Bien Phu

Hanoi ★
Haiphong •

Haiphong
Harbor •

Hainan

BURMA

Gulf of Tonkin

LAOS

Mekong R.

Mu Gia
Pass

supply
route

the DMZ
(demilitarized
zone 1954)

17th parallel

Khe Sanh
Quang
Tri Province

Hue

Tet
Offensive

Da
Nang

Chu Lai

THAILAND

Dak To

Ho
Chi
Minh
Trail

Pleiku

Central
Highlands

KAMPUCHEA
(Cambodia)

Mekong R.

SOUTH
VIETNAM

Phnom
Penh ★

An Loc

Xuan
Loc

Kompong
Som •

Mekong R.

Saigon
(now Ho Chi Minh City)

Mekong
Delta

Gulf of Thailand

South China Sea

Date	Action
Aug. 4, 1964 . .	Pres. Johnson announced U.S. destroyers attacked in Gulf of Tonkin.
Aug. 7, 1964 . .	Congress approved Tonkin Gulf Resolution, increasing U.S. involvement in Vietnam.
1965–1973 . . .	U.S. air raids on supply routes.
Jan. 30, 1968 .	Tet Offensive begins. North Vietnam attacks major cities of South Vietnam.
Mar. 1972	North Vietnam began a major invasion of South Vietnam. Nixon ordered the mining of Haiphong harbor.
Jan. 27, 1973 .	Cease-fire arranged. Last American ground troops left Vietnam two months later.
late 1974	North Vietnamese and Vietcong capture Phuoc Long.
March 1975 . .	Vietcong force South Vietnamese troops to retreat from Central Highlands. Retreat became known as the Convoy of Tears.
Apr. 30, 1975	South Vietnam surrendered. Saigon renamed Ho Chi Minh City.

0   100   200 Miles

0   200 Kilometers

▲ Battles

One

★

ASSASSINATIONS AND CONNECTIONS

Countless Americans can vividly recall their reactions on November 22, 1963, when they heard the announcement that President John F. Kennedy had been shot and killed. For some it was a devastating and life-altering experience. The world became a very unfriendly place, and it seemed there was no longer anything like "security" in American life. For days most Americans sat in front of a television set, witnessing the funeral of a man many considered a friend and experiencing the transition of power that took place in the most powerful nation on earth.

Just three weeks earlier, another national leader in an obscure corner of Southeast Asia was assassinated. President Ngo Dinh Diem of South Vietnam had been in power since 1954. A coup d'état (violent overthrow) led by the country's military on November 1, 1963, forced him into hiding. The military agreed to give him safe passage out of the country. An armored car was sent to take Diem and his brother to a rendezvous with the new leaders. But the car stopped at a railroad crossing, and the men were quickly shot—executed without ceremony.

Public reaction in Vietnam to the death of Diem was in stark contrast to the U.S. mass mourning for the loss of a president. Some Vietnamese rejoiced at Diem's murder, but his death had hardly any impact on the lives of the Vietnamese peasant population who struggled just to survive on their small family farms. Peasants had little hope that their lives would improve with a change of government.

THE VIETNAM AND U.S. CONNECTION

What was the connection between two entirely different nations and their leaders who were murdered within weeks of each other? During the 1960s, it was not readily apparent. Most Americans were focused on domestic concerns such as the emerging civil rights movement and widespread social changes in the country. But some people closely watched events in Vietnam, particularly if members of their families were in the military or were Korean War veterans. U.S. troops were part of the United Nations forces that had been sent to Korea during the 1950s to stop communist aggression in Asia.

Even before the Korean conflict, U.S. actions planted the seeds of U.S. involvement in Vietnam, bringing forth an unwelcome harvest. The Vietnam era, as it is called, was one of the nation's most painful periods.

FIRST STEPS INTO THE QUAGMIRE

Long before that era, in 1857, the French sent troops into Indochina to protect missionaries who were attempting to convert the Southeast Asian masses to Christianity. Eventually, the French colonized three Indochinese nations—Laos, Cambodia, and Vietnam—and set up strategic military bases in Asia, gaining access to many goods and raw materials. But there was a cost. Ho Chi Minh, a native of Vietnam educated in Paris, France, was inspired in 1929 to establish a communist organization to fight against the foreign control of his homeland. His Indochinese Communist Party, which in 1941 became the Viet Nam Doc Lap Dong Minh, or the Viet Minh for short, was the dominant force for liberation on the Indochinese peninsula.

During World War II, Germany occupied France, so the French were unable to defend their Southeast Asian colonies from a Japanese takeover. Although Ho Chi Minh was pleased that the French were weakened in his homeland, he had no intention of allowing power to be transferred to the Japanese. With the help of U.S. weapons and training, he continued his resistance against the forces trying to control his land.

Ho Chi Minh was a leader in the
Vietnamese fight for independence from France.

By the time Japan surrendered to the United States in August 1945, the Viet Minh had formed a coalition with other Vietnam communist groups. With a weakened French and Japanese presence in their country, the Viet Minh seized the opportunity to control the government. On September 2, 1945, the Democratic Republic of Vietnam declared independence.

U.S. officials had supported the Viet Minh efforts because during World War II the Japanese were more of a threat than the communists. But after the war, policies changed. The United States did not want a communist government to maintain power. Thus, even though President Harry S. Truman was opposed to helping another country continue its colonization effort, the United States offered aid to France, a longtime ally.

THE "FIRST" VIETNAM WAR

In an effort to regain control of their colony, the French landed troops in Vietnam on September 24, 1945. French leader General Phillipe Leclerc announced that he was there to reclaim what belonged to France and, in effect, instigated the first Vietnam War. Three months later the Viet Minh attacked French forces in the north. General Leclerc, looking at the obvious superiority of the modern French ground forces, boldly declared that his men would defeat the Viet Minh in four weeks.

However, the French vastly underestimated the Viet Minh and did not heed the warnings of Bao Dai, the Vietnamese emperor who had gone to live in France. The emperor advised the French that no one would be able to restrain the Vietnamese yearning for independence. "Should you re-establish a French administration here, it will not be obeyed. Every village will be a nest of resistance, each

The Viet Minh had very few cannon. This one was captured from the French in 1945.

former collaborator an enemy, and your officials and colonists will themselves seek to leave this atmosphere, which will choke them."[1]

Relying on guerrilla warfare, the Viet Minh used stealth and surprise to gain advantage over their heavily armed enemies. Skirmishes between the Viet Minh and the French occurred in various places in Vietnam during most of 1946, and a full-scale war was underway by November. Seven and a half years later, in May 1954, the Viet Minh finally brought the mighty French army to its knees at the Battle of Dien Bien Phu.

THE DOMINO THEORY

In the United States, the Truman administration was convinced that communism was a monolithic evil inspired by the regime in the Soviet Union, which planned on world domination. Advisers such as Dean Rusk, the undersecretary of state, urged the president and the U.S. Congress to provide financial support for the French effort in Vietnam. According to Rusk, the purpose of such assistance was to preserve "Indochina and Southeast Asia from further Communist encroachment."[2] At the same time, the United States also sent troops to counter an invasion of Soviet-backed invaders in Korea. These efforts were the result of what was known as the domino theory, first described during World War I but popularized by President Dwight D. Eisenhower when a reporter asked about the importance of Indochina to the free world. Eisenhower replied that there were broad considerations

> that might follow what you would call the "falling domino" principle. You have a row of dominoes set up, you knock over the first one, and what will happen to the last one is the certainty that it will go over very quickly. So you could have the beginning of a disintegration that would have the most profound influences.[3]

According to the theory, unless Asian countries received help from the United States, they would eventually fall under communist (Soviet and Chinese) domination, one after another. Because of the domino theory, the U.S. military became bogged down in a no-win situation in the rugged hills of Korea for four years.

When President Truman committed troops to the Korean War under United Nations auspices in 1950, the United States also provided $15 million in military aid to the French forces in Vietnam. In addition, thirty-five U.S. military advisers went to Vietnam to help train the local troops. These advisers were the first of a long line of American military personnel who would come to know just where this obscure piece of Asia was located.

In hindsight, this policy of containment, driven by the belief that the North Koreans or the Viet Minh were taking their marching orders directly from the Soviets or the Communist Chinese, was terribly flawed. The Vietnamese and Chinese were, in fact, traditionally bitter enemies. When the United States, acting out of concern about the spread of communism, refused to recognize the legitimacy of the government of Ho Chi Minh in 1945 and backed the recolonization effort of the French, the Viet Minh leader had little choice in his pick of allies. The Chinese recognized his government. These were different times.

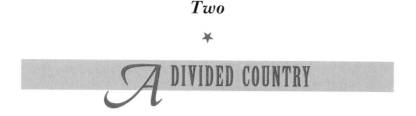 A DIVIDED COUNTRY

After Ho Chi Minh defeated the French in Dien Bien Phu in 1954, a conference was held in Geneva, Switzerland, to bring about an end to the French–Viet Minh conflict. The result was a temporary truce, with the country partitioned into two nations at the 17th parallel. An election to unify the country was supposed to be held in 1956.

In the north, Ho Chi Minh's communist forces were dominant, so they controlled that section of the country. The Republic of South Vietnam was established in the south with Ngo Dinh Diem as president.

Representatives of the United States and the South Vietnam governments refused to sign the Geneva agreement because they believed the communists would try to control all of Vietnam. South Vietnam, in fact, denounced the Geneva pact and protested the partitioning of the country. Both the U.S. and South Vietnamese representatives, however, promised not to use force to oppose the cease-fire. But the U.S. representative cautioned that the United States would be concerned about any renewal of aggression and see it as a threat to international peace and security. He also said the United States would encourage unity through free elections, which would be supervised by the United Nations so voting would be conducted fairly.

*Ngo Dinh Diem, president of the Republic of South Vietnam, broadcast
an appeal for army unity several months after taking office in 1955.*

The French and Viet Minh ended their fighting, and
the French were forced to begin withdrawal, finally terminating their long rule over the country. South Vietnam was
granted full independence, and in accordance with the
Geneva agreement, many communist sympathizers moved
north while thousands of refugees, many of them Catholic,
fled south (with the aid of the U.S. Navy) to escape the communists.

DICTATORS

In 1956, Diem, backed by the United States, refused to hold elections at the specified time. U.S. officials feared that the South Vietnamese president, who was proving to be a very inept leader, would be handily voted down in favor of Ho Chi Minh and the Communist Party candidates.

Political enemies of Diem in the south and north were incensed by Diem's flagrant abuse of power. Many in the south banded together to form a people's militia known as the Vietnamese Communist, or Viet Cong. Receiving support from the Viet Minh and the North Vietnamese government, as well as the Soviet Union and Communist Chinese governments, the Viet Cong began using the proven tactics of guerrilla warfare to undermine the South Vietnamese government and the Diem regime.

A Catholic in an overwhelmingly Buddhist country, Diem placed many members of his family in positions of power, including his brother, who directed the military to suppress the Buddhist majority. Because Diem was dictatorial, life for the common person was no better than it had been before Diem became their leader. In many ways there was more equality under the Viet Minh.

The U.S. government feared that the South Vietnamese would never be victorious against the Viet Cong attacks. A U.S. State Department official expressed his concerns in a 1955 memo:

> I am still convinced Diem does not have the knack of handling men nor the executive capacity truly to unify the country and establish an effective government. If this should become evident, we should either withdraw from Vietnam . . . or we should take such steps as can legitimately be taken to secure an effective new premier. . . . Throughout all this I

feel we must keep our eyes clearly on our main objective in Vietnam, i.e., to assist in saving this country from communism.[1]

Ho Chi Minh, as a leader of North Vietnam, certainly had his faults, too. After his regime took control, a brutal land reform program was put into motion. Thousands of former landowners and other capitalists were placed in forced-labor prison camps. Many other thousands were simply executed so that their farmland could be redistributed to the peasantry, who had hardly been better off than slaves for countless generations. Ho Chi Minh eventually admitted the mistakes of that time, but other Viet Minh leaders contended that Communist Chinese advisers had pushed them into the program.

ENDING DIEM'S RULE

From 1950, when the first U.S. military advisers were sent to support the training of the Army of the Republic of Vietnam (ARVN), the Military Assistance and Advisory Group continually increased. By the end of 1962, there were over 11,000 U.S. advisers in Vietnam, escalating to 16,000 the following year. Some actually took part in sporadic fighting against the Viet Cong guerrilla attacks. The United States also sent funds, which totaled well over $1 billion from 1955 to 1961.

President Kennedy's administration was fully committed to seeing that communism was stopped in Vietnam. In his inaugural address, he had given notice to every nation that "we shall pay any price, bear any burden, meet any hardship, support any friend, oppose any foe to assure the survival and success of liberty."[2] His speech focused on American military strength and the U.S. commitment to a fight against communism.

However, by 1963, Kennedy was impatient and frustrated with President Diem's actions. Diem continually defied demands of the Kennedy administration to make governmental reforms, and he resisted having U.S. combat troops in South Vietnam. Instead, Diem relied on a tactic known as the strategic-hamlet program. In order to prevent guerrillas from hiding in villages, he "relocated" entire communities, putting villagers into hamlets surrounded by stakes or moats and under ARVN guard.

In many instances, the Diem government also discriminated against Buddhists and arrested numerous clergy and students. The clergy went into the streets to protest in 1963. In one highly dramatic incident Quang Duc, a monk in Saigon, was doused in gasoline by a fellow Buddhist, then burned alive as he sat in the middle of a busy street. Other monks passed out leaflets with Quang Duc's plea for the Diem government to allow religious freedom. The incident was captured on film and shown to television audiences in the United States and throughout the world; it was the first of a series of such suicides.

When it became clear that Diem and his brother had no intention of modifying their policies, Kennedy's advisers suggested withdrawing aid and making contact with alternative leaders who could take over. According to the official position, the United States did not want to "stimulate coup," yet neither did it want to give the impression that the administration "would thwart a change of government or deny military assistance to a new regime if it appeared capable of increasing effectiveness of military effort."[3]

However, the Central Intelligence Agency (CIA) backed the coup attempt of the South Vietnamese military, especially when conflict between the Diem government and the Buddhist monks escalated. Although American officials agreed to make Diem "expendable," President Kennedy did not support the assassination of Diem and his brother.

Diem's death, as a result of the coup, did little to stabilize the situation in South Vietnam. A continual series of coups and countercoups kept the government from any effective leadership for many months. In this power vacuum, the North Vietnamese and the Viet Cong decided to step up their attacks on South Vietnam and ARVN facilities.

After President Kennedy was assassinated, Lyndon Johnson became president and inherited the Vietnam problem. To contain the communists, Johnson believed more men and supplies would be needed *in country*, a term that came to represent American military duty on Vietnamese soil. This Americanization of the war became ever more clear to the U.S. public as events of the first week in August 1964 unfolded.

GULF OF TONKIN INCIDENTS

On August 2, 1964, Commodore John J. Herrick, commander of a task force of four U.S. destroyers that made coastal patrols, was aboard one of the ships, the *Maddox*, which Captain Herbert L. Ogier commanded. The *Maddox*, apparently on routine patrol, headed for the Gulf of Tonkin, a bay off the coast of North Vietnam. Other naval vessels were supporting commando raids by the ARVN on nearby islands.

Although the *Maddox* was not part of that support group, the North Vietnamese thought the destroyer was the coordinating vessel of the raids and launched three patrol torpedo (PT) boats into international waters. "The next thing we knew they came at us," Herrick reported.[4]

It was 3:08 P.M. when Herrick, as ranking officer, validated Captain Ogier's order to open fire on the attacking boats. As the PTs took evasive action, they launched torpedoes at the *Maddox*. All of the water missiles missed their mark, while gunfire from the deck of the *Maddox* made a hit on one of the attackers.

U.S.S. Maddox *firing its cannons at attacking*
PT boats in the Gulf of Tonkin, August 2, 1964

"Commodore Herrick watched the battle by radar,"
according to one journalist's account. "On the scope he
could see the shells exploding and boats coming." Herrick
later revealed that "one thought kept going over and over in
my mind. . . . 'It can't be happening.'"[5]

In minutes, four American jets swooped down in support of the U.S. Navy destroyer with its canons blazing. The
attack, which lasted about twenty minutes, was broken off,
and the *Maddox* steamed to safer waters.

Two nights later, asserting the right to sail without harassment in international waters, the U.S. government ordered the return of the *Maddox* to the Tonkin waters. This time it was accompanied by a second destroyer, the *Turner Joy*, and overhead support aircraft. At 9:30 P.M., in a pitch-black stormy night, suspicious blips were reported on the radar screens of both warships. While there is some controversy over whether or not the blips really represented enemy ships attacking, the *Maddox* and the *Turner Joy* fired their guns and took evasive action for thirty minutes. They then resumed regular patrol.

After the second incident, President Johnson ordered retaliation against the North Vietnamese PT bases. Johnson wanted to be seen as a decisive leader in the eyes of an electorate about to vote for their next president, so he rushed to a decision before making absolutely sure that the second attack on U.S. warships actually happened. Commodore Herrick himself was unsure, and he had communicated his misgivings to his superiors. But Johnson wanted to act. Just prior to midnight on August 4, 1964, he appeared to the nation on television, announcing that North Vietnam had deliberately attacked U.S. naval vessels. "Repeated acts of violence against the armed forces of the United States must be met not only with alert defense, but with positive reply," he said. "That reply is being given as I speak to you tonight."[6]

THE U.S. RESPONSE

The U.S. responded with air raids against four Vietnamese PT boat bases and a major oil depot. The attack was successful, but two U.S. aircraft were lost and one young pilot paid a severe price. Lieutenant Everett Alvarez Jr. took off from the aircraft carrier *Constellation* on orders to bomb a patrol-boat base.

I was among the first to launch off the carrier . . . headed toward the target four hundred miles away. . . . It was sort of like a dream. We were actually going to war, into combat. I never thought it would happen, but all of a sudden here we were, and I was in it. I felt a little nervous. We made an identification pass, then came around and made an actual pass, firing. I was very low, just skimming the trees at about 500 knots. Then I had the weirdest feeling. My plane was hit and started to fall apart, rolling and burning. I knew I wouldn't live if I stayed with the airplane, so I ejected, and luckily I cleared a cliff.[7]

Alvarez broke his back in the landing, but he survived and was captured, the first of almost 600 pilots who became prisoners of war (POWs) in the North Vietnamese camps. Alvarez was held prisoner under horrible conditions until the end of the war some eight years later.

On August 5, President Johnson delivered a message to the U.S. Congress saying that "the North Vietnamese regime has given a new and grave turn to the already serious situation in southeast Asia." He reminded Congress that a treaty obligated the United States "to meet Communist aggression" and that "America keeps her word." A "threat to any nation in [Asia] is a threat to all, and a threat to us," the president said. Then he asked the Congress "to join in affirming the national determination" and assist "the free nations of the area to defend their freedom."[8]

Within a few days Congress passed the Tonkin Gulf Resolution by a unanimous vote in the House and with only two dissenting votes in the Senate. It stated in part that the U.S. Congress supported "the determination of the President, as Commander in Chief, to take all necessary measures to repel any armed attack against the forces of the United States and the Charter of the United Nations."[9]

President Johnson speaks from the White House on
August 10, 1964, at the signing of a congressional resolution
backing a firm stand against aggression in Southeast Asia.

The resolution was not a formal declaration of war, but
war is what it meant. Full of confidence and secure in the
notion that America would make things right, the government of the United States decided to ignore the lessons of
the French and to plow headlong into the Southeast Asian
quagmire.

Three

★

INCREASING AMERICAN INVOLVEMENT

United States involvement in the war gained real impetus on February 7, 1965, when the Viet Cong boldly attacked an American barrack at Pleiku, killing 8 men and wounding 126. President Johnson's national security adviser, McGeorge Bundy, was in Saigon that day and drafted a memo that would become U.S. policy in regard to the enemy:

> We believe that the best available way of increasing our chance of success in Vietnam is the development and execution of sustained reprisal against North Vietnam. . . . While we believe that the risks of such a policy are acceptable, we emphasize that its costs are real. It implies significant U.S. air losses even if no full air war is joined, and it seems likely that it would eventually require an extensive and costly effort against the whole air defense system of North Vietnam.[1]

The first implementation of this new war tactic in Vietnam began on February 24 with limited but massive air-bombing runs against targets north of the 17th parallel. These attacks were part of a plan known as Operation Rolling Thunder to punish the north for helping the Viet Cong in the south and to stop the VC, or Victor Charlies, as they were sometimes called, from overrunning the South Vietnamese government.

General William Westmoreland talking with some of his troops in South Vietnam

After President Johnson appointed General William Westmoreland to head the Military Assistance Command, Vietnam (MACV), the general called for additional troops to help protect the new air bases being built. By June there were 75,000 U.S. troops on Vietnamese soil. In July 1965, President Johnson told the American people that the United States would provide the general with whatever he needed, and by the end of the year almost 200,000 troops were in the country.

WAR OF ATTRITION

Westmoreland was convinced that "normal" warfare could not succeed in Vietnam. From ages past, and even up to the last conflict in Korea, opposing armies had fought to control strategic areas of terrain. The army that captured and/or controlled the most important land was the winner. In the case of Vietnam, however, the general's men took a village during the day, then as soon as they left at night, the Viet Cong came back to take control. So Westmoreland decided to fight a war of attrition—to kill an increasing number of enemy soldiers, count the bodies, and publicize the toll of dead to try to demoralize the North Vietnam forces.

It was the job of the grunt, a nickname given to the infantryman, to carry out the search-and-destroy tactics. The foot soldier had to slog through mud, dodge mines and booby traps, avoid snipers, and find village strongholds of the VC. As a defense, the Viet Cong and villagers sympathetic to the communists invented numerous lethal traps to snare Americans, such as grenades triggered by hidden wires and hidden pits with sharply pointed bamboo sticks that could pierce the body. In villages, mines were often hidden under the mud floors of huts. According to one U.S. government study, between January 1967 and September 1968, nearly 24 percent of American casualties were caused by booby traps and mines.[2]

Once a village was captured, the American soldiers destroyed any food, supplies, and weapons that might be of use to the VC in the future. When they could find the guerrillas, they captured and killed them. By the end of 1966, 400,000 American troops were in the country attempting to get as many "kills" as they could. But the communist forces kept coming back, infiltrating the south at a steady rate of 7,000 per month.

THE HUMAN MOLES

In spite of superior weapons and aircraft and billions of dollars poured into their effort, U.S. forces could not "control" the land in South Vietnam. In the history of warfare, there probably has never been an army better at fighting by stealth than the Vietnamese guerrillas. For one thing, Americans did not understand until much later that the Viet Cong were living and thriving in an elaborate system of tunnels that honeycombed under the very sites that American forces had "secured." After the war, General Westmoreland explained in his memoirs that "no one has ever demonstrated more ability to hide his installations than the Viet Cong; they were human moles."[3]

One example of how the "human moles" operated was evident in the region around the village of Cu Chi, located within twenty-five miles of Saigon, the capital of South Vietnam. (Today it is actually part of greater Saigon renamed Ho Chi Minh City at the end of the war.) As early as the 1940s, when the original Viet Minh were striking out at the French, the Vietnamese had dug many miles of tunnels. Then in the 1960s, the Viet Cong set up a base of operations in the area, and as Ba Huyet, a Viet Cong guerrilla, recalled,

> the first thing we did was to start digging thirty kilometers of underground tunnels. . . . Not only was this one of our closest outposts to Saigon, but it was our advanced command post throughout the war. The Americans were sure something was going on here, but they were not sure what.[4]

Americans, who seemed to be fighting an invisible enemy, bombed and napalmed the Cu Chi area more often than any other theater of the war. By the early 1970s, hardly any vegetation could be seen growing on what used to be a verdant plain with rice paddies, rubber plantations, family farms, and junglelike growth.

One reason for the continued bombing was to prevent men and supplies from moving down the famous Ho Chi Minh trail, a communist supply line that skirted the western border of Vietnam from the north, winding through Laos and Cambodia and ending in Cu Chi. Americans wanted to foil attempts of the communists to establish a stronghold near Saigon. But the incredible destruction aboveground was undermined by the tunnels below.

A typical Viet Cong tunnel complex was an intricate array of pathways, shafts, and dug-out caves that resembled a highly systematized city. There were workshops for making arms and ammunition, hospitals, sleeping quarters, and even kitchens equipped with remote chimney outlets that would take the telltale smoke hundreds of yards from the actual location of the men hidden underground. Although these tunnel cities were almost directly under the noses of the American reconnaissance (recon) patrols, only on occasion would U.S. troops find a tunnel entrance. Then a volunteer was sent in to survey and/or destroy what he could.

THE RECON PATROL

"The most potentially dangerous job was that of Recon Platoon Leader," wrote Ulf R. Heller, a young grunt who spent a year and a half in Vietnam. His reconnaissance platoon, which included South Vietnamese troops, was on one patrol when, as Heller recalled, the troops suddenly

> began shooting into the ground and hollering. They had found a possible air hole for a tunnel. We pushed smoke grenades into the hole and looked for other places where the smoke came out. It was kind of scary waiting for a Viet Cong to jump out of a hole. We pulled one dead guy out of a hole. He was dyed violet from the smoke grenade . . . [and] he had a tooth missing. Evidently one bullet had knocked out the tooth and buried itself in his body without exiting.

Infantrymen who had the dangerous job of exploring Viet Cong tunnels were called "tunnel rats." A tunnel rat was a specially trained shorter-than-average GI.

Heller's patrol also attempted to combat the Viet Cong by "trying to ferret out the bad guys" in villages. The platoon patrolled the roads in jeeps, which were, in Heller's words,

loaded down with a M-60 machine gun on a pedestal mount, sand bags on the floor for mines and what we called the toy boxes which were mortar ammunition boxes full of explosives. . . . A piece of angle iron was welded to the front bumper. It was higher than a sitting man and the last six inches were notched and angled forward. It was designed to cut wire that might be stretched across the road and designed to decapitate someone driving in a jeep with its windshield down.[5]

Other American recon patrols searched along jungle trails at night, sometimes with their faces blackened to make themselves less visible in what little light existed. Jeff Drake was on his first combat patrol, moving deep into the jungle, when the sounds of birds and other jungle creatures seemed to stop abruptly. With extreme caution, the men inched forward. Suddenly there was an explosion, and Drake thought he was in the midst of an ambush. But there was no gunfire. A mine had been tripped, and the next thing he heard was a man screaming, "Mama, Mama!"

Drake and a buddy with him were able to get to the source of the screams, expecting at any time to set off another mine. Their relief at being safe quickly turned to horror as they saw one of their patrol on the ground. Drake described the wounded man's condition as if seeing him for the first time:

> Both his knees are bent 90 degrees in the wrong directions and his fatigues appear to have hundreds of holes in them. Through the holes, blood is spurting everywhere. He must have severed arteries, because the blood acts like it's being pumped. I had no idea people could bleed like that. His screams have turned to moans, and I feel like I'm going to pass out as the others gather around us.[6]

Four

*

QUESTIONING THE REASONS FOR WAR

"Here in Vietnam the war goes on," one officer wrote in a letter to his brother in 1967. "Morale is very high in spite of the fact that most men . . . believe we will *not* win the war. And yet they stick their necks out every day and carry on with their assigned tasks as if they were fighting for the continental security of the United States. Hard to believe, but true."[1]

As historical records show, most U.S. military personnel in Vietnam were more than willing to fight because their country asked them to. Loyalty and pride and a sense of nationalism have always been important factors in waging a war, and the American men and women in Vietnam were as patriotic as any in previous U.S. conflicts. They were told repeatedly that they had to prevent the advance of evil communism. "Better to stop the aggression in Southeast Asia than on the beaches of California" was a typical argument. Very few of the young people, whose average age was only nineteen years, knew anything about the long struggle of the Vietnamese people for independence.

MORALITY ISSUES

In spite of patriotic fervor, the war was also a confusing and miserable time for many in the U.S. military. Scared and often unsure of who the enemy really was, soldiers trusted very few Vietnamese and frequently operated by the "mere gook" rule—they were trained to think of the Vietnamese as less than human, thus not covered by the international law that required the protection of civilians in the time of war and the humane treatment of prisoners. They learned to kill Vietnamese by any possible means.

U.S. troops in jungle fighting also became calloused by the unspeakable atrocities against American prisoners who were tortured by the Viet Cong. One witness to an atrocity was Arthur E. Woodley Jr. After he joined the army, he volunteered "for the toughest combat training they had." As he reported, "I went to jump school, Ranger school, and special forces training. I figured I was just what my country needed. A black patriot who could do any physical job they could come up with."[2] Woodley became a combat paratrooper with the Fifth Special Forces Group of the 173rd Airborne Division.

During one recon mission, Woodley and the team he led came across an American soldier who had been captured, skinned alive, and staked to the ground. The mutilated soldier pleaded to be shot—he wanted someone to end his ordeal. Woodley called headquarters for help, but he was told there was no way to get the man out or to bring in medical aid. It was Woodley's responsibility to decide what to do. "It took me somewhere close to 20 minutes to get my mind together," he reported. "Not because I was squeamish about killing someone, because I had at that time numerous body counts." But he did not think he could kill an American GI. Still as he listened to the agonized pleas of the tortured man, who was near death, Woodley felt the only right thing to do was to pull the trigger. "I cancelled his suffering." His team buried the soldier without a word. "Then I cried," Woodley reported.[3] Ever since, he has had recurrent nightmares over this act.

The Vietnamese were not alone in their brutality. American fighting men also committed atrocities, as the U.S. public learned several years later when a U.S. Senate committee investigated war crimes in Vietnam. John Kerry, a Vietnam veteran who became a U.S. senator from Massachusetts, testified that numerous highly decorated veterans told horror stories about what they had done. Kerry reported:

> [at] times they had personally raped, cut off ears, cut off heads . . . limbs, blown up bodies, randomly shot at civilians, razed villages . . . shot cattle and dogs for fun, poisoned food stocks, and generally ravaged the countryside of South Vietnam in addition to the normal ravage of war.[4]

The kind of incidents Kerry described were certainly not characteristic of all U.S. troops in Vietnam. Lieutenant Colonel John McGarrahan recalled that when he was a captain in Vietnam he

> commanded a company in Long Binh, about thirty miles away from Saigon. Often I would lead large truck convoys from Long Binh out to remote locations to resupply American and South Vietnamese units. The convoys would pass through villages of all sizes, frequently stopping to wait for escorts. I enjoyed watching the soldiers as they interacted with the people of the village. They found their way around the language barrier, they teased the girls, they joked with the older people, they played with the little kids and shared candy or other goodies with them. At the same time they had to be very wary, just in case a person who looked friendly turned out to be a Viet Cong soldier.
>
> That does not mean there were no atrocities, but I never saw anything of that sort during the year that I was in

Vietnam. When American soldiers go off to war, they take all the strengths and weaknesses of their characters with them. When there is good discipline, when there is effective teamwork in the unit, and when there is good leadership, those strengths shine and the weaknesses stay under control.[5]

THE WAR AT HOME

Whatever atrocities and loss of discipline that occurred, the incidents were partly a result of the "body count" mentality of some American officials. The war of attrition called for creating a favorable ratio of American to Viet Cong dead. By the end of the war, more than two million Vietnamese lost their lives while American deaths were placed at just over 50,000. But the killing had a terrible effect on those watching from the safety of their homes back in the United States.

On their favorite TV news programs, Americans could see the graphics and charts that tracked the weekly number of dead and over the years followed the progress of what was called the "first TV war." Reporters on the scene at a Vietnamese city or village would show the bloody wreckage of what was left after a firefight, interview a GI about how much longer he had before he was coming home, or show what looked like the surface of the moon as a result of the spraying of the defoliant Agent Orange. TV reports usually ended with graphics of small coffins on the screen, each one equal to one hundred dead soldiers.

As the war entered many American living rooms, opinions about whether to continue the fighting began to shift, although concerted protests had emerged as early as 1965. Some historians and others who have chronicled the Vietnam War blamed early protests on radicals and communist factions within the United States. But countless ordinary

Agent Orange was widely sprayed in Vietnam
to defoliate the dense jungle growth.

citizens opposed the continuation of a war that seemed to stem from an immoral base. Rather than trying to control land, which made killing appear to be a necessary evil, the U.S. military now seemed intent on "killing to kill," an idea abhorrent to many Americans. Pacifist groups—including Quakers, who lived by a nonviolent philosophy and condoned no wars—were especially saddened by U.S. actions. They were among the first to rally against the Vietnam conflict.

The protest of one young Quaker, Norman R. Morrison, had a profound effect on Robert McNamara, the defense secretary from 1961 to 1968. McNamara was the chief architect of the war in the Kennedy and Johnson administrations, and he recalled one of the first major antiwar protests on November 2, 1965:

> At twilight that day . . . Morrison, father of three and an officer of the Stoney Run Friends Meeting of Baltimore, burned

Property of Dexter
Middle School Library

himself to death within 40 feet of my Pentagon window. When he set himself on fire he was holding his one-year-old daughter in his arms. Bystanders screamed, "Save the child!" and he flung her out of his arms. She survived.[6]

Later that month another Quaker, emulating the Buddhist monks of South Vietnam, burned himself alive in front of the United Nations building in New York City. Several other protest suicides followed.

STUDENT ANTIWAR PROTESTS

The antiwar movement in the United States built up momentum from 1966 through 1967. Protesters staged marches and spoke out in public forums and in the media. There was no central authority or single leader of this grassroots movement that brought together people from very diverse backgrounds. In October 1967, thousands of antiwar activists, including clergy, pacifists, and writers, marched on the Pentagon in Washington, D.C., demonstrating against this symbol of military power.

Numerous college students were especially opposed to the use of the draft to fill the ranks of the military units performing service overseas. They were incensed when the Johnson administration established a policy to make students with low grades some of the first to be eligible for the draft.

At the same time, there were those on campus who joined the army's Reserve Officers Training Corps (ROTC). Vietnam veteran John McGarrahan was in the ROTC during his years at Wheaton College (1963–1967), in Wheaton, Illinois, and recalled:

Because of the Vietnam War, many of my college friends thought that since they would very likely be going into military service as soon as they graduated from college, they would rather serve as officers. However, other friends were opposed to the war; and they planned to take their chances on being drafted, declared their conscientious objection or chose professions such as the ministry to avoid service. I can still remember vividly an ROTC parade during my senior year. The cadets marched in formation through the campus to the football field for a ceremony, then marched back. As we marched by in each direction, a number of my friends stood along the road and held large cardboard signs declaring their objection to what was going on in Vietnam and to the actions of the United States military there. But both the cadets marching and their fellow students protesting were still able to come together for dinner in the dining hall in mutual respect that evening.[7]

Stan Koper, who was on campus at the University of Michigan from 1965 through 1969, was, in his words

opposed to the war, because I knew it was a mistake, and I didn't want to be sent to fight it. . . .

I remember the society in which we were living seemed upside down—crazy. The war seemed to be craziest of all.

My hobby is military history. . . . In military history, you find example after example of massive [snafus], and the worst part is, people are needlessly killed as a result.

Koper "also sympathized with the people drafted into the war. I knew . . . that it was difficult for people to go against their own government, particularly when it didn't seem evil or obviously, totally wrong about the war."[8]

On campus and elsewhere, draft-card burnings, flag burnings, teach-ins, more mass marches, rallies, and flights to Canada to avoid the draft were some of the tactics employed by "doves" who wanted peace and opposed the

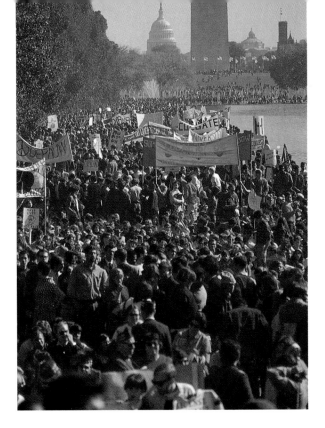

A demonstration in Washington, D.C.,
protesting the Vietnam War

war aims of the "hawks." The hawks pushed for more troops and continued bombing of North Vietnam. Some even talked about using the atom bomb, and they supported General Westmoreland whenever he called for more troops and supplies.

In November 1967, the general went on television to say that enemy strength had declined and to express optimism for success in 1968. Privately, he asked the president for 100,000 more men so he could end the war in three years. Three months later, before the president could agree, the Viet Cong showed just how strong they really were.

Five

✦

A VIOLENT YEAR

$\mathcal{T}$et was the most important holiday of the year in Vietnam, a lunar new year celebration that was like Christmas and Thanksgiving rolled into one. Both sides had agreed to a truce so that soldiers could go home to be with their families. Robert Parrish, a young army lieutenant assigned to work with an ARVN unit, noted:

> Everything seemed normal for the holiday season—except something kept nagging at me. Many of the travelers were young men of military age. This wasn't particularly unusual, because we had been authorized to allow fifty percent of our troops to go on leave.... [But] quite a few of the young men were in civilian clothes—not the normal dress for off-duty ARVN soldiers—and they weren't carrying Tet gifts.[1]

The reason for Parrish's "nagging" feeling soon became clear. VC soldiers used the Tet holiday truce to infiltrate positions for a major surprise attack on the strongholds in South Vietnam. The Tet Offensive, as it was called, had been planned for months, and preliminary staging had been accomplished in the bases of the north, across the border in Cambodia, and in the tunnel complexes, especially at Cu Chi. On January 30, 1968, the Viet Cong sent masses of soldiers to attack provincial and district capitals and major cities. Saigon was overrun with enemy troops, and some even broke into the U.S. embassy compound.

A few days after the outbreak of the offensive, Lieutenant Parrish, with an ARVN unit, was in a firefight in the city of Phu Cuong, just north of the capital. "It was pretty obvious that the VC were there to stay and that this wasn't going to be a picnic," he recalled. "As we carefully made our way along the main east-west street, we began to see evidence of the recent fighting."

The company eventually encountered a battalion of Viet Cong who pinned down Parrish's small eighty-man unit. Parrish reported:

> Those of us near the road began to crawl forward, while the others darted from one building to the next. The VC increased their fire, but most of their rounds were passing over our heads. . . . Since we couldn't move forward and wouldn't pull back, we just had to wait until we got reinforcements or new orders. There wasn't anything else to do, so I decided to play sniper. . . . a Viet Cong suddenly appeared—right in my sight. He was creeping forward along the edge of a building 150 meters directly to my front. I squeezed the trigger, and when I looked again, I could see the soles of his Ho Chi Minh sandals.[2]

THE TURNING POINT

Using B-52 bombers and infantry grunts to take back captured towns street by street, building by building, the American forces with the help of the ARVN finally shut down the estimated 65,000-man Tet Offensive. The goal of the offensive had been to prompt a popular uprising, but that never materialized. The allies killed more than 40,000 of the enemy, while relatively few American lives were lost.

Militarily the allied defense could be considered a vic-

American forces often had to fight street-by-street
to recapture towns during the Tet Offensive.

tory. In the United States, however, TV audiences during early 1968 watched battles for supposedly secure cities. Americans had been assured by General Westmoreland that there was light at the end of this long tunnel. Now it seemed that much more effort would be needed to put down an enemy that did not know the meaning of defeat.

In addition, soon after U.S. and ARVN troops took control of Saigon once again, an especially grisly scene appeared on TV and in newspapers across the country. Photographs were taken at the very moment the chief of the South Vietnamese police, General Nguyen Ngoc Loan, pulled the trigger on a pistol held to the head of a bound Viet Cong prisoner. Many viewers were outraged and disgusted by the act. As one war historian explained:

> The pictures captured what was most disturbing about the war to many Americans: the disparity between the bare-footed bound prisoner and the general, with his flak jacket, his heavy American pistol, the callous indifference to consti-tuted rules of war; the terror of death meted out in America's name, with American means, by men like Loan.[3]

When an all-time weekly high of U.S. casualties was set on February 17, 1968, with 543 killed and 2,547 wounded in action, an increasing number of Americans, including many members of Congress, began to declare that the war was unwinnable. Fighting no longer seemed in the best interest of their country.

In short order, several other events affected the course of the war. General Westmoreland asked for 206,000 more troops to be sent to Vietnam. Secretary McNamara, now dis-illusioned with the choices he had made in support of esca-lating the U.S. involvement, lobbied hard against that request. He also suggested to a congressional committee that the massive bombing of North Vietnam, which accounted for more tonnage of explosives than all the bombs dropped on Europe in World War II, was having little effect on the enemy. In the end, he resigned his position, and Westmore-land only got a few thousand more troops. The new secre-tary of defense, Clark Clifford, announced a policy change: "Vietnamization" of the war, which meant ARVN forces would be required to assume more responsibility.

Another major change was in store for the nation. On March 31, 1968, President Lyndon Johnson told the American public that he could "not permit the presidency to become involved in the partisan divisions that are developing in this political year. . . . Accordingly, I shall not seek, and I will not accept, the nomination of my party for another term as your president."[4]

The president's party had revolted against the way he was running the war, and it was obvious that his chances for reelection were slim. He decided to concentrate on finding an honorable way to end the fighting, which at the time had taken the lives of almost 30,000 Americans. Johnson cut back bombing raids on the north, limiting flights to below the 20th parallel, and called for peace negotiations to begin.

The North Vietnamese sent delegates to peace talks in Paris, France, but they quickly insisted that all bombing had to stop if negotiations were to continue. Johnson agreed, which gave a boost to the presidential candidacy of his vice president, Hubert Humphrey, who was challenged in the Democratic primaries by Robert Kennedy, brother of slain President John F. Kennedy.

BLOODBATHS AT HOME

By early 1968, the United States seemed to be tearing apart. Violence had erupted in many parts of the United States during civil rights and antiwar demonstrations. To many blacks, as well as other Americans, the fighting in Vietnam seemed not only senseless but immoral, and civil rights leaders, led by the Reverend Martin Luther King Jr., had been speaking out strongly against the Vietnam War.

In April 1968, Dr. King was assassinated, and riots

flared in black neighborhoods across the United States as people vented their rage with the slogan "Burn, baby, burn!" Some black soldiers in Vietnam who had fought side-by-side with whites, in spite of numerous instances of racism, began to seriously rethink their role in the war. Communist propagandists took advantage of the situation, urging blacks to go home because the war was really a capitalist trick to kill them off. "The loyalty of the black Vietnam War veteran stood a greater test on the battleground than did the loyalty of any other American soldier," wrote journalist Wallace Terry, who covered the war for *Time* magazine.[5]

College and high school students boycotted classes in protest over the war and King's death. At Columbia University students occupied five buildings on campus to demonstrate their animosity toward university officials who supported the war.

Just two months later, on June 4, Robert Kennedy was shot by Sirhan Sirhan, who opposed Kennedy's support of Israel. Kennedy died two days later. After his death, Hubert Humphrey became the top candidate for presidential nominee at the Democratic National Convention, which was held in Chicago in August. Many antiwar activists opposed Humphrey's nomination because he supported Johnson's policies. Thousands of demonstrators converged on Chicago to protest the war, among them traditional religious pacifists as well as radical protesters, including members of the Students for a Democratic Society and a group known as the Youth International Party, or Yippies, who called for a violent revolution.

Radicals planned to disrupt the Chicago convention and threatened to burn down the city and kidnap delegates. This was a serious threat to Chicago Mayor Richard J. Daley, who called for thousands of police and National Guard support. Protesters taunted police, calling them Nazi pigs and

Demonstrators protesting the war clash with police outside the Democratic National Convention headquarters in 1968.

other derogatory names, and pelted them with everything from bottles to urine-filled balloons. Police lost control and turned on the demonstrators, wildly clubbing people, sometimes even those who were merely passing by or were on hand to report events.

As Americans saw the scene unfold on TV, many were outraged once more, particularly those who thought that U.S. military efforts should be supported. Some no doubt shifted their political loyalties to the Republican Party and its nominee Richard Nixon, who won the 1968 election by a slim margin.

Six

✦

NO END IN SIGHT?

By the beginning of 1969, a new Viet Cong offensive was on the horizon. The North Vietnamese had amassed more than 40,000 men and many fresh supplies in neutral Cambodia, just across the South Vietnamese border. Advisers to newly inaugurated President Nixon, including General Creighton Abrams, who replaced Westmoreland as MACV commander, thought there should be a short-duration bombing of Cambodia even though civilians would likely be injured or killed.

Hamstrung by President Johnson's earlier agreement not to bomb in North Vietnam in order to keep the peace talks on line, Nixon and his security adviser Henry Kissinger, were anxious to demonstrate that they would negotiate only from a position of strength. Nixon quickly agreed to bomb Cambodia but insisted that it be a top secret mission. He knew there would be adverse public reaction if Americans learned that U.S. planes were attacking a neutral nation and that the war was expanding. The bombing lasted for four-teen months, but it actually failed in its goal to intimidate the communists.

All the while, peace talks continued in Paris with very little progress. Neither side was willing to give much ground at the negotiating table. As a result, secret talks began between Henry Kissinger and the formidable North

Vietnamese representative Le Duc Tho, the man responsible for the continuing Viet Cong attacks. Nixon believed that results could only be achieved through these talks.

Still there was no letup in the fighting in Southeast Asia. Even though there was no established frontline, U.S. troops fought on a great variety of battlefields, from jungles to hamlets to city streets, and in the air with bombers and helicopters. And search-and-destroy missions were still routine, although more of the duties were being forced upon the South Vietnamese army. With Vietnamization, the U.S. military presence began to diminish. But by the end of 1969, there were still more than 475,000 Americans on Vietnamese soil.

MEDEVAC

Among those in Vietnam were thousands of women who made up a critical part of the support team of medical experts, as well as special services positions and clerical jobs. Other women were civilians with the Red Cross and other volunteer organizations or were reporters and photographers on assignment. An estimated 33,000 to 55,000 military and civilian women worked in Vietnam during the war.

While military women did not see combat, they experienced the hell of war, working near the battle zones as highly skilled health practitioners in Medical Evacuation (Medevac) teams. Most were part of the nursing personnel at Evac hospitals, which were located no farther than an hour's helicopter ride from a battlefield.

The "Huey" (HU-1, Bell) and other multipurpose helicopters were an integral part of the operation of this war. Many of the 36,000 missions involving helicopters were started with a "Slick," the name for a helicopter flying low, doors wide open, to hover over a "hot LZ" (landing zone under fire) so a squad of infantrymen could jump to the ground

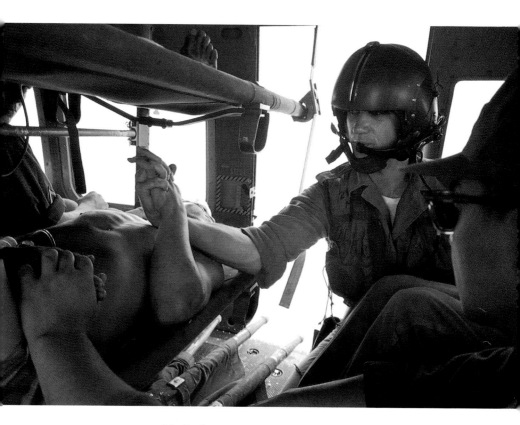

Medical personnel aboard a medevac
helicopter comfort a wounded soldier.

below. The Slick was also used as a "dustoff" vehicle for medevac recovery missions, which were instrumental in transporting 98 percent of the American battlefield wounded into an Evac hospital.

Twenty-year-old Christine Schneider worked at the Ninety-fifth Evac Hospital in Da Nang in 1970 and recalled what it was like when the Medevac copters arrived:

> nothing could prepare you for the horrible things you saw . . .
> these big Chinook helicopters came in, and the corpsmen

> went out and got all these guys. I remember one of the nurses saying, "You take him." I'll never forget him because he was my first one. . . . He was wide awake even though half his face was gone, and he was scared. I remember cutting off all his clothes and the horror of taking one of his boots off and his foot still being in the boot.[1]

Another nurse, Lily Jean Lee Adams, had been against the war when she was in nursing school, but she wanted to do something for her country. So she joined the army, expecting to aid wounded and maimed soldiers coming back from Vietnam. Instead she was ordered to the Twelfth Evac Hospital in Cu Chi and was assigned to the intensive care unit.

One of her first jobs was to watch over a nineteen-year-old North Vietnamese Army prisoner of war (POW). While she was caring for him, a group of interrogators came in to ask the man some questions. Adams explained:

> I was listening to all these questions, kind of enjoying learning more about my patient. Then I said to the interrogator, "Would you do me a favor? Would you ask him a question from me?" And he said, "Sure, what is it?" I said, "He doesn't have to answer if he doesn't want to, but I'd like to know how he feels about the war." The interpretation was—and he looked straight at me when he said it—"If I could march in Hanoi, like you are marching in Washington, D.C., I would be doing it."[2]

MORE PROTESTS AT HOME

Americans were indeed marching in Washington. After the secret bombing of Cambodia was leaked to the press in 1969, another series of protests began, but it was the "moratorium" movement that had the greatest impact. It was initiated by Sam Brown, a former campaigner for Democratic presidential candidate Eugene McCarthy, who opposed the war. Brown helped organize local, community-based demonstrations to widen the protest from the college campuses and involve working folks in their own neighborhoods.

The first moratorium was held October 15, 1969, with the largest demonstration in Washington, D.C., where 250,000 people followed Coretta Scott King in a candlelight vigil through the city. New York, Boston, Miami, and other cities heard distinguished and respected Americans like Dr. Benjamin Spock and Ambassador Averell Harriman speak out against continuing the terrible conflict. The next moratorium a month later on November 15 was even larger. Almost 300,000 people took to the streets of the nation's capital.

WAR CRIMES REVELATIONS

During the time of the moratorium demonstrations, several news reports were published about a young, inexperienced U.S. army officer, Lieutenant William Calley, who was being investigated for his role in a massacre of Vietnamese civilians. At first, the stories created little stir in the United States, but in November 1969, major newspapers carried a series of articles written by Seymour Hersh, a former Associated Press reporter. Hersh had interviewed Calley and others under his command in C (or Charlie) Company who had participated in an assault that had occurred more than a year earlier along the northeastern coast of South Vietnam in a small village called My Lai.

Hersh's articles, and later his book based on interviews with at least fifty participants, explained that several platoons of C Company were ordered to destroy a Viet Cong battalion known to be in the area. Calley and his platoon of twenty-five men were the first to be dropped by helicopters near the village; they were followed by two other platoons.

As Calley's troops entered the hamlet on the morning of March 16, 1968, no one fired on them and villagers were peacefully attending to their daily routines. But Calley and his men rounded up women, children, the infirm and elderly—and began killing them. Calley himself gathered a group of about eighty villagers and ordered one of the men in the platoon, Paul Meadlo, to "waste them." As Meadlo reported: "We stood about ten to fifteen feet away from them and then he [Calley] started shooting them. Then he told me to start shooting them. So we went ahead and killed them."[3]

By all accounts, Calley and the men of C Company lost any semblance of control, as did the other platoons who committed countless atrocities from gang rapes to brutal mutilations of civilians. Calley's men began lobbing grenades into huts and then firing their M-16s at the villagers. Some Vietnamese were marched to a drainage ditch and machine-gunned. Between 350 and 500 unarmed villagers were murdered during that day of rampaging.

After the story of the massacre was finally revealed, it was soon followed by published photos, reproduced from color slides taken by an army photographer, Ronald Haeberle, who had been present at the time. The pictures showed piles of bodies, scenes of crawling wounded children, and terrified villagers just before they were killed. When some members of Congress viewed the original slides, they were literally sickened.

Calley and several others in Charlie Company were charged with murder, but only Calley was convicted by court-martial. This stirred further controversy in the United States as many Americans believed Calley was a scapegoat for his superiors, while others thought he deserved severe punishment for his barbarous acts. Because of the intervention of President Nixon, Calley served only a short sentence under house arrest.

VIOLENCE ON THE HOMEFRONT

The revelations of My Lai shocked many Americans who had never believed that U.S. soldiers would commit war crimes in Vietnam. Some became even more disillusioned when Nixon once more escalated the fighting. Early in 1970, the president promised to bring home an additional 150,000 troops by year's end, while at the same time he ordered an excursion into Cambodia to chase out North Vietnamese troops who had found a sanctuary there. The action lasted only a couple of months, but the reaction on U.S. campuses was immediate and intense. Some colleges and universities closed down when faculty joined students in protest.

On April 30, 1970, President Nixon went on television to explain to the nation his decision to send troops into Cambodia.

Violent confrontations with the authorities took place at Kent State University in Ohio. On May 4, 1970, thousands of protesting students were confronted by inexperienced National Guardsmen called up to maintain the order by Governor James Rhodes, who likened the students to "brownshirted Nazis." In the panic that ensued, dozens of students were injured and four were killed. Not long afterward at Jackson University in Florida, two students lost their lives in a confrontation with the police.

Marchers again descended on Washington, D.C. Among them was Ron Kovic, a Vietnam veteran who lost the use of his legs in the war. He became an antiwar activist and wrote about his experiences in a popular book, *Born on the Fourth of July* (which later became a movie). As he described it, "I was sitting alone in my apartment listening to the radio when I first heard the news about Kent State. . . . For a moment there was a shock through my body. I felt like crying. . . . I remember saying to myself, The whole thing is coming down now."[4]

Even the U.S. Congress asserted itself by symbolically terminating the Tonkin Gulf Resolution, the only legal justification for pursuing the war. But throughout 1971 the pace of the fighting remained consistent, with thousands of Vietnamese and Americans still losing their lives. Nixon continued to bring troops home, however, turning more of the fighting over to the ARVN, who had some success in controlling the region in and around the Mekong Delta. By Easter of 1972, there were less than 95,000 Americans left in the country, only 6,000 of them combat ready. Peace talks were going nowhere, and the North Vietnamese decided to take this opportunity to launch a major new offensive.

Seven

★

A BITTER END

Within a month of the Easter offensive, Henry Kissinger and Le Duc Tho were able to work out a secret agreement that would remove American troops, return POWs, and provide for a political settlement in Vietnam. But the president of South Vietnam, Nguyen Van Thieu, who had ruled since 1967, refused to certify the agreement on October 24, 1972. Nixon supported him because the agreement favored the Viet Cong, allowing them and North Vietnamese troops to remain in the south. The North Vietnamese were very upset and publicized details of the secret negotiations, accusing the United States of backing out of the agreement. Henry Kissinger put the best spin on the situation when he spoke to reporters, however, saying, "We believe that peace is at hand. We believe that an agreement is within sight."[1]

On November 7, Americans went to the polls to reelect Richard Nixon by a huge plurality over Democrat George McGovern. Most of them were convinced that the war would finally come to an end. And the Paris talks did resume soon after the election. But they broke down completely on December 13 when Le Duc Tho returned to Hanoi and refused to compromise on the issue of removing his troops from the south at the start of any cease-fire agreement.

Angered by the North Vietnamese, Nixon refused to

resume talks and ordered a massive series of bombing raids against the North on December 18. Led by U.S. B-52 bombers, American pilots dropped more than 40,000 tons of bombs on military and civilian areas north of the 17th parallel through January 30, 1973. Twenty-six aircraft were downed in the more than 3,000 missions flown during the Christmas bombings, and sixty-two aviators were killed. Another thirty-one were added to the long list of POWs that began with Lieutenant Everett Alvarez Jr. in 1964.

POWS

During the hostilities, more than 700 Americans, mostly air force and navy pilots, were held in prisoner-of-war camps and prisons located within thirty-five miles of Hanoi. Twenty-three died in places nicknamed the Hanoi Hilton, the Zoo, Alcatraz, the Plantation, and the Powerplant. And by most accounts given by POWs after they were finally freed, their lives were a living hell during the internment.

Jeremiah Denton took off from an aircraft carrier in the Gulf of Tonkin on July 18, 1965, on a mission to bomb one of the most heavily defended bridges in all of North Vietnam. His plane was hit at least twice by antiaircraft fire, and he was forced to eject over enemy territory. Captured as soon as he reached the ground, he was transported to the Hanoi Hilton and later transferred to the Zoo, where he was marked for special tortures because he would not cooperate with his captors.

For many days Denton received only meager food rations sprinkled with tiny bits of human fecal matter. When the North Vietnamese tried to get him to provide biographical information that they would use for propaganda purposes, he still would not oblige them. They decided to take a more severe approach. "Although I had been starved, humiliated, left without medical care, and placed in irons, I wasn't quite prepared for what was to happen next," wrote Denton in his memoirs. He was taken into a blacked-out room by a man called Smiley, "a tough, efficient guardsman much feared by the prisoners." The guard hooked him into cuffs that held his arms behind his back and cut deeply into his wrists.

> Smiley asked me if I would write. "No," I said. He raised his arm suddenly, striking me flush in the face with his fist and knocking me down. As I looked up dazedly, he reached down, pulled me up, and hit me again several times.

The beatings went on at irregular intervals for at least four days. In between visits by Smiley, Denton was left to fend for himself, manacled in the pitch-black cell that had no heat during the bitterly cold nights. As an act of defiance, he decided not to eat the food that was brought in to him twice each day. Soon he was hallucinating from lack of nutrition, lack of light, and the pain now radiating from his arms and wrists.

> On what I believed was the fourth night, Smiley checked my cuffs. . . . He gave a little grunt and departed. . . . In a few minutes he was back with some tools. . . . Smiley was worried. My wrists were torn and bleeding, and so swollen that he couldn't contract the cuffs enough to disengage the ratchets and remove them. By squeezing very hard, he finally got one cuff off, but the other was buried deep in the pus-filled flesh.

The guard finally removed the other cuff from his wrist, and Denton was able to see that his "fingers were black and swollen to twice their normal size." But this was not to be the end. Smiley found a larger set of cuffs, put them on, and shut off the light once more in Denton's room. Three days later, delirious to the point of raving, he yelled for the guards. "The next thing I remember was [a guard] forcing a pen into my fist. Painfully, I wrote a biography."[2]

A PEACE AGREEMENT

America's continued intense bombing compelled the North Vietnamese to restart the talks on January 8. At the same time, the U.S. Congress refused to provide funds for further American military action in Vietnam. In January 1973 the Paris Accords were signed, and the twenty-three year involvement of the United States in Vietnamese affairs began to end. American soldiers, like Ulf Heller, boarded planes to go home.

Le Duc Tho signed the cease-fire
agreement in Paris on January 23, 1973.

We were a fairly subdued lot, but when the pilot announced that we were leaving Vietnamese airspace, we started cheering. The next thing I knew I was in the San Francisco Airport. . . . My mother had sent a green uniform to the airport Holiday Inn so I wouldn't freeze in my khakis. I changed and went to the restaurant to eat a good steak. I automatically reached into my back pocket and snapped open my Buck knife with one hand to cut my steak. The sound of the knife opening echoed through the room and everyone looked at me with my knife in the air. I really felt like a fool. My war was over.[3]

Marines wait to board the plane taking them home at the end of the war.

But many American soldiers faced another type of battle on the home front. Some were greeted with overt hostility. As Patrick Gray of Bellevue, Nebraska, recalled:

> When I came back from Vietnam I was dumb enough to wear my dress uniform in the San Francisco International Airport. This was on April 15, 1970. A nicely dressed woman in her twenties blocked my path and hissed "God-damned murderer" in my face. I guess guys who lose a war get pretty unpopular.[4]

Because of the unpopularity of the war and the traumatic experiences of many soldiers in Vietnam, the war is still like an open wound for some Americans. An estimated 40 percent of the homeless in the United States are Vietnam veterans, and an undetermined number of Vietnam veterans have developed cancers from the defoliant Agent Orange and other chemical weapons used during the war. Organized groups that include families of men missing in action continue to search for information about the remains of American soldiers or those who might still be POWs.

The war also "has created doubts about American judgment, about American credibility, about American power— not only at home, but throughout the world. It has poisoned our domestic debate," noted Henry Kissinger, the former secretary of state and the chief negotiator for the United States at the peace talks that finally ended the hostilities. He concluded, "We paid an exorbitant price for the decisions that were made in good faith and for good purpose."[5]

Source Notes

One

1. Quoted in Stanley Karnow, *Vietnam: A History. The First Complete Account of Vietnam at War*—A companion to the PBS TV series (New York: Viking, 1983), 147.

2. Quoted in Harry Nickleson, *Vietnam* (San Diego: Lucent Books, 1989), 19.

3. Quoted in William Appleman Williams, et al., eds., *America in Vietnam: A Documentary History* (Garden City, N.Y.: Anchor Press/Doubleday, 1985), 156.

Two

1. Quoted in John Clark Pratt, *Vietnam Voices: Perspectives on the War Years, 1941–1982* (New York: Viking Penguin, 1984), 61–62.

2. Quoted in Thomas C. Reeves, *A Question of Character: A Life of John F. Kennedy* (New York: The Free Press, 1991), 233.

3. Quoted in Guenter Lewy, *America in Vietnam* (New York: Oxford University Press, 1978), 27.

4. Quoted in Karnow, *Vietnam*, 368.

5. Quoted in Eugene G. Windchy,*Tonkin Gulf* (New York: Doubleday), 123.

6. Quoted in Lester A. Sobel, ed., *South Vietnam: U.S.-*

Communist Confrontation in Southeast Asia, Vol. 1 1961–1965 (New York: Facts on File, 1966), 116.

    7. Quoted in Karnow, *Vietnam*, 373.

    8. Remarks included in Joint Resolution of Congress, H.J. RES 1145 August 7, 1964, Department of State Bulletin, August 24, 1964, electronic posting <gopher://wiretap.spies.com:70/11/Gov/US-History/Vietnam>

    9. Ibid.

Three

    1. Quoted in Pratt, *Vietnam Voices*, 187.

    2. Lewy, *America in Vietnam*, 309.

    3. Quoted in Tom Mangold and John Penycate, *The Tunnels of Cu Chi* (New York: Berkley Books, 1986), 15.

    4. Ibid., 24.

    5. Ulf R. Heller, "Images of My War, Recon Platoon," 1994, on REMEMBRANCES Home Page, July 14, 1995, <http://grunt.space.swri.edu/vnbk08.htm>

    6. Jeff Drake, "Claymore Alley," REMEMBRANCES Home Page, 1994, <http://grunt.space.swri.edu/claymore.htm>

Four

    1. Bernard Edelman, ed., *Dear America* (New York: Pocket Books, 1985), 209.

    2. Quoted in Wallace Terry, *Bloods: An Oral History of the Vietnam War by Black Veterans* (New York: Random House, 1984), 244–245.

    3. Ibid., 248.

    4. John Kerry. "Vietnam Veterans Against the War Statement to the Senate Committee of Foreign Relations," April 23, 1971.

    5. Personal correspondence with Kathlyn Gay, February 23, 1996.

6. Robert S. McNamara. "We Were Wrong, Terribly Wrong," *Newsweek* (April 17, 1995), 46.

7. Personal correspondence with Kathlyn Gay, February 23, 1996.

8. Stan Koper. Electronic posting on "Emi's Online Antiwar Anthology" maintained by Dennis Snow <http://ftp.std.com/Emi.Anthology/intro.html>

Five

1. Robert D. Parrish, *Combat Recon: My Year with the ARVN* (New York: St. Martin's Press, 1991), 164.

2. Ibid., 171–183.

3. Marilyn B. Young, *The Vietnam Wars 1945–1990* (New York: HarperPerennial, 1991), 225.

4. Quoted in Karnow, *Vietnam*, 523.

5. Terry, *Bloods*, xvii–xviii.

Six

1. Keith Walker, *A Piece of My Heart* (Novato, Ca.: Presidio Press, 1985), 38.

2. Ibid., 320.

3. Quoted in Seymour M. Hersh, *My Lai 4: A Report on the Massacre and Its Aftermath* (New York: Random House, 1970), 50.

4. Ron Kovic, *Born on the Fourth of July* (New York: McGraw-Hill, 1976), 120.

Seven

1. Quoted in Nickelson, *Vietnam*, 67.

2. Jeremiah A. Denton, *When Hell Was In Session* (Clover, S.C.: Commission Press, 1976), 62–67.

3. Heller, "Images of My War."

4. Quoted in Bob Greene, *Homecoming: When the Soldiers Returned from Vietnam* (New York: G. P. Putnam's Sons, 1989), 232.

5. Karnow, *Vietnam*, 21.

For Further Information

Books

Barr, Roger. *The Vietnam War.* San Diego: Lucent Books, 1991.

Becker, Elizabeth. *America's Vietnam War: A Narrative History.* New York: Clarion Books, 1992.

Brown, Gene. *The Nation in Turmoil: Civil Rights and the Vietnam War (1660–1973).* New York: Twenty-First Century Books, 1994.

Denenberg, Barry. *Voices from Vietnam.* New York: Scholastic Paperbacks, 1995.

Devaney, John. *The Vietnam War.* New York: Franklin Watts, 1992.

Dolan, Edward F. *America After Vietnam: Legacies of a Hated War.* New York: Franklin Watts, 1989.

Edwards, Richard. *Vietnam War.* Vero Beach, Fla.: Rourke, 1987.

Hass, Marv E. *Women's Perspectives on the Vietnam War.* Pittsburgh: Center for Social Studies, 1991.

Kent, Deborah. *The Vietnam War: "What Are We Fighting For?"* Springfield, N.J.: Enslow Publishers, 1994.

Lawson, Don. *The United States in the Vietnam War.* New York: Harpercrest, 1981.

Lens, Sidney. *Vietnam: A War on Two Fronts.* New York: Lodestar Books, 1990.

Marrin, Albert. *America and Vietnam: The Elephant and the Tiger.* New York: Viking, 1992.

Myers, Walter D. *A Place Called Heartbreak: A Story of Vietnam.* Chatham, N.J.: Raintree Steck-Vaughn, 1992.

Warren, James A. *Portrait of a Tragedy: America and the Vietnam War.* New York: Lothrop Lee & Shepard, 1996.

Wormser, Richard L. *Three Faces of Vietnam.* New York: Franklin Watts, 1993.

Wright, David K. *The Story of the Vietnam Veterans Memorial.* Chicago: Childrens Press, 1989.

A/V and CD-ROM

Air Power in Vietnam: The U.S. Air Force in Vietnam (videocassette, 50 min.). New York: Good Times Home Video, 1987. Early U.S. buildup in Vietnam from 1964–1969; role and functions of the U.S. Air Force in the Vietnamese conflict. Grades 5–8.

Vietnam: A Visual Investigation (CD-ROM). Redmond, Wash.: Medio Multimedia, ©1994. Multimedia information about the Vietnam War. Grades 7 and up.

Vietnam, a Television History (7 videocassettes). New York: Sony Corporation of America, ©1983. Thirteen-part documentary that chronicles three decades of struggle in Vietnam. Grades 7 and up.

Index